THE **STATE GOVERNOR**

by Martha E. H. Rustad

STATE

GOVERNOR

PEBBLE
a capstone imprint

Pebble Explore is published by Pebble, an imprint of Capstone.
1710 Roe Crest Drive
North Mankato, Minnesota 56003
www.capstonepub.com

Library of Congress Cataloging-in-Publication data is available on the Library of Congress website.
ISBN 978-1-9771-1391-7 (hardcover)
ISBN 978-1-9771-1817-2 (paperback)
ISBN 978-1-9771-1401-3 (ebook pdf)

Summary: Describes a governor's duties, how they are elected, where they work, and more.

Image Credits
Alamy: caia image, Cover, ZUMA Press Inc, 19; Library of Congress Prints and Photographs, 26; Newscom: Reuters/Carlos Barria, 23, Sipa USA/Alex Milan, 17, TNS/Mark Mirko, 9, ZUMA Press/Bruce R. Bennett, 5, ZUMA Press/Michael Brochstein, 14; Shutterstock: Everett Historical, 24, f11photo, 21, Glam 7 (right), Krista Kennell, 28, Krylovochka, 7 (left, middle), mark reinstein, 13, Nagel Photography, 27, Paul Brady Photography, 22, Rich Koele, 25, Rob Crandall, 15; U.S. Marine Corps photo by Staff Sgt Jason W. Fudge, 10

Design Elements
Shutterstock: ExpressVectors, soponyono

Editorial Credits
Anna Butzer, editor; Cynthia Della-Rovere, designer;
Jo Miller, media researcher; Laura Manthe, production specialist

Printed and bound in China.
2489

Table of Contents

Words in **bold** are in the glossary.

What Is the Governor?

What if you had a job where you call the shots? In bad weather, you can cancel school. At the state fair, you can give a speech. Your office is in your state's **capital** city. In an emergency, you can call the U.S. president. Every day you help people. Only 49 other people have the same job as you.

Who are you? The governor of your state!

A governor gives a speech as part of his job.

A governor is the leader of a U.S. state. A governor works for a state's government. This is a group of people that help a state run well. Each state's government has three branches, or parts. Each part has a different job.

The first part is the **executive branch**. The governor works in this part. The second part is the **legislative branch**. State lawmakers write laws and rules for their state. The third part is the **judicial branch**. State courts check that rules and laws are fair for everyone.

State Government

Executive

Leads State Government

Governor

Legislative

Writes Bills

House of Representatives

Senate

Judicial

Decides What Laws Mean

State Supreme Court

Federal Courts

Who Can Be a Governor?

Do you want to be the governor of your state? Each state has its own rules about who can be governor.

Most state governors must be U.S. **citizens**. People are citizens if they are born in the United States. Some people come from other countries. They may choose to become U.S. citizens. They take a test and make a promise to the country.

A governor must live in the state he serves.

Many states say that the governor must live in that state. Some states say the governor must have lived in the state for a certain amount of time.

In most states, people must be a certain age to be governor. But some states do not have any rules about the governor's age.

Some states have odd rules about governors. In Hawaii, the governor cannot have any other jobs.

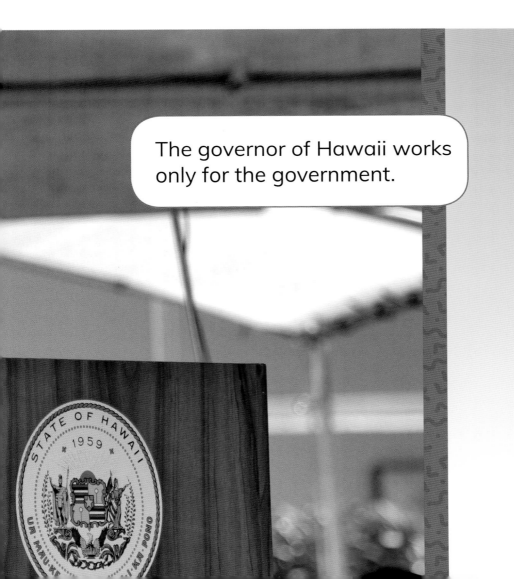

The governor of Hawaii works only for the government.

How Governors Are Chosen

People in each state choose their governor. Citizens can **vote** when they are 18 years old. They mark their votes on **ballots**.

A **candidate** is someone who wants to be governor. Candidates ask to be on the ballot. The rules for being on a ballot are different in each state.

STATE GOVERNOR

Candidates talk to people. They travel all over their states. They listen to what people want. They tell people how they will help.

Candidates talk to people about their plans.

People vote on **Election** Day. The candidate with the most votes wins! The winner becomes governor after a few months.

Most governors work for a **term** of four years. In Vermont and New Hampshire, governors work for a term of two years.

At the end of a term, people must vote again. Some states have rules for how many times a person can be governor.

People vote for their governor.

What Do Governors Do?

The governor is the leader of a state. The governor's main job is to make sure people follow the state's laws.

The governor reads **bills** from state lawmakers. The governor signs a bill to make it a law. A governor can **veto** a bill. That means the governor does not think it should be a law.

A governor also makes a state **budget**. This is a plan for how to spend money. Lawmakers can make changes to the plan. In some states, the governor chooses state **judges**.

A team of people help a governor work. They write speeches, answer letters, and talk to people.

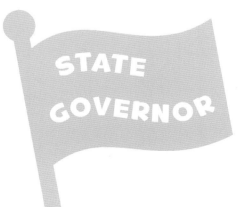
STATE GOVERNOR

Where Do Governors Work?

The governor works in the state's capital city. It holds many of a state's government buildings. State lawmakers and judges also work in there.

In some states, the governor works in the capitol building. Each state's capitol building looks different.

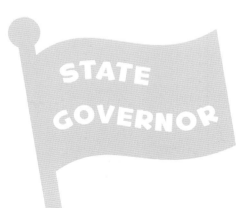

STATE GOVERNOR

Colorado's state capitol

Some states have a house for their governor. A governor might live in this house.

MISSOURI
GOVERNOR'S MANSION
BUILT 1871

A governor might meet with the president to talk about ideas.

Governors travel to all parts of their states. They give speeches. They listen to the state's citizens.

Governors meet with other leaders in the capital. They talk about ways to help people.

Famous Governors

GOVERNOR OF TWO STATES

Sam Houston is the only person to be a governor in two states. He served Tennessee from 1827 to 1829. He was the governor of Texas from 1859 to 1861.

LONGEST GOVERNOR'S TERM

Terry Branstad was a governor for a total of 22 years. He was governor in Iowa from 1983 to 1999. He was elected again from 2011 to 2017.

FIRST FEMALE GOVERNOR

Nellie Tayloe Ross was the first woman to be governor in the United States. She was the governor of Wyoming from 1925 to 1927.

SHORTEST GOVERNOR'S TERM

Hiram Bingham III was the governor for the shortest time. He served Connecticut for only one day in 1925.

FROM GOVERNOR TO PRESIDENT

Seventeen people have been both a state governor and U.S. president. Thomas Jefferson was governor of Virginia. Theodore Roosevelt served as the governor of New York. George W. Bush was the governor of Texas before becoming president.

George W. Bush

ACTORS AND GOVERNORS

Some famous actors became governors. Arnold Schwarzenegger has been in more than 30 movies. He was California's governor from 2003 to 2011.

Arnold Schwarzenegger beginning his second term as California's governor.

Fast Facts

STATE GOVERNOR

Role: The Governor

Job: Governors work for the citizens of their state. The governor checks that people follow the state's laws.

How Governors Are Chosen: Voters in each state choose a governor. They vote every two or four years. Each state has different rules about how long a person can be governor.

Pay: Governors earn different amounts in each state. The pay ranges from $70,000 to almost $200,000.

Glossary

ballot (BAL-uht)—a list of candidates from which voters choose

bill (BIL)—a proposed law introduced in Congress

budget (BUH-juht)—a plan for spending money

candidate (KAN-duh-dayt)—a person who wants a job in government

capital (KA-puh-tuhl)—a town where a state's government buildings are

capitol (KA-puh-tuhl)—a building where state government workers do their jobs

citizen (SI-tuh-zuhn)—a member of a country

election (i-LEK-shuhn)—the act of choosing people to work in government

executive branch (ig-ZE-kyuh-tiv BRANCH)—this branch makes sure people follow rules and laws

judge (JUHJ)—a person who is in charge of a court room and gives decisions in some cases

judicial branch (joo-DISH-uhl BRANCH)—courts and judges make sure rules and laws are fair

legislative branch (LEJ-iss-lay-tiv BRANCH)—lawmakers write rules and laws for people to follow term (TERM)—a set amount of time for a job

veto (VEE-toh)—to choose not to sign a bill into law

vote (VOHT)—a choice made by a person based on their own views

Read More

Manning, Jack. *The State Governor*. North Mankato, MN: Capstone Press, 2015.

Murray, Julie. *Governor*. Minneapolis: Abdo Kids, 2018.

Nagelhout, Ryan. *Standing in a Governor's Shoes*. NY: Cavendish Square Publishing, 2016.

Internet Sites

How Stuff Works: State Governor
https://people.howstuffworks.com/government/local-politics/state-governor.htm/printable

State Capitol Buildings
http://50statesinalphabeticalorder.com/Capitol%20Buildings.htm

U.S. State Capitals: Facts for Kids
https://kids.kiddle.co/List_of_U.S._state_capitals

Index